I Know Someone with Cancer

Cancer

Sue Barraclough

Heinemann Library
Chicago, Illinois

www.heinemannraintree.com
Visit our website to find out more information about Heinemann-Raintree books.

To order:

☎ Phone 888-454-2279

💻 Visit www.heinemannraintree.com to browse our catalog and order online.

© 2011 Heinemann Library
an imprint of Capstone Global Library, LLC
Chicago, Illinois

All rights reserved. No part of this publication may be reproduced or transmitted in any form or by any means, electronic or mechanical, including photocopying, recording, taping, or any information storage and retrieval system, without permission in writing from the publisher.

Edited by Rebecca Rissman, Daniel Nunn, and Siân Smith
Designed by Joanna Hinton Malivoire
Picture research by Mica Brancic
Originated by Capstone Global Library
Printed in the United States of America by Worzalla Publishing

14 13 12 11 10
10 9 8 7 6 5 4 3 2 1

Library of Congress Cataloging-in-Publication Data
Barraclough, Sue.
  I know someone with cancer / Sue Barraclough.
    p. cm. — (Understanding health issues)
  Includes bibliographical references and index.
  ISBN 978-1-4329-4564-0 (hc)
  ISBN 978-1-4329-4580-0 (pb)
  1. Cancer—Juvenile literature. I. Title.
  RC264.B37 2011
  616.99′4—dc22   2010026580

Acknowledgments
We would like to thank the following for permission to reproduce photographs: Alamy p. 25 (© Stephen Lloyd UK); Corbis pp. 14 (© Fabio Cardoso), 17 (Sygma/Micheline Pelletier), 19 (© Kevin Dodge), 25 (© Stephen Lloyd UK), 26 (epa/© Gero Breloer); Getty Images pp. 15 (Photographer's Choice/Mark Harmel), 16 (Stone/David Joel); Photolibrary pp. 6 (cell division in 3d), 7 (BSIP Medical/Raguet H), 12 (age fotostock/Frank Siteman), 13 (Jacky Chapman), 18 (BSIP Medical/Godong/Deloche), 20 (Kablonk! Kablonk!), 23 (Stockbroker), 24 (Cultura/Christine Schneider), 27 (Tim Rooke); Science Photo Library pp. 8 (Moredun Animal Health Ltd), 9 (Power and Syred); Shutterstock pp. 4 (© Yuri Arcurs), 5 (Margot Petrowski), 10 (Gertjan Hooijer), 21 (© Sean Prior), 22 (Monkey Business Images).

Cover photograph of a cancer patient reproduced with permission of Getty Images (Taxi Japan/ULTRA.F).

We would like to thank Matthew Siegel and Ashley Wolinski for their invaluable help in the preparation of this book.

Every effort has been made to contact copyright holders of any material reproduced in this book. Any omissions will be rectified in subsequent printings if notice is given to the publisher.

All the Internet addresses (URLs) given in this book were valid at the time of going to press. However, due to the dynamic nature of the Internet, some addresses may have changed, or sites may have changed or ceased to exist since publication. While the author and publisher regret any inconvenience this may cause readers, no responsibility for any such changes can be accepted by either the author or the publisher.

Contents

Some words are printed in bold, **like this**. You can find out what they mean in the glossary.

Do You Know Someone with Cancer?

You might know someone who has been sick with cancer. People with cancer might have treatment for a long time to make them fit and healthy again.

Someone who has cancer may have to spend a lot of time in the hospital.

Cells are too small to see, but they make up every part of your body.

Cancer is a type of illness that affects the **cells** in the body. Cells are tiny living parts that fit together to make your body.

What Is Cancer?

Most **cells** in the body grow and divide all the time. This growth and change is controlled. This means it starts and stops to do a particular job, such as making new cells or healing cells that have been damaged.

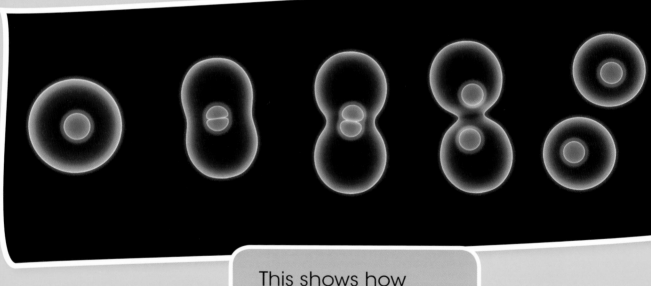

This shows how normal cells divide and grow.

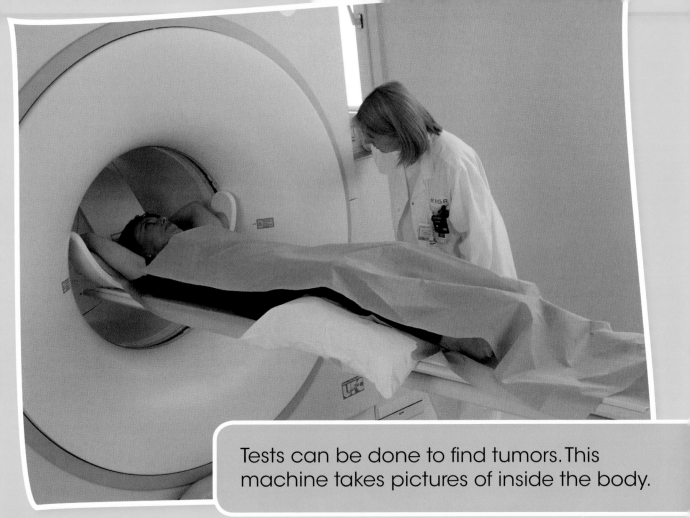

Tests can be done to find tumors. This machine takes pictures of inside the body.

Cancer is when cells start to grow out of control and divide too fast. Groups of cancer cells can cause growths called **tumors**. A tumor is a swelling or a lump caused by cells growing out of control.

Tumors happen inside the body and cannot always be seen from outside the skin.

tumor

If a **tumor** is not treated, it can grow so big that it stops body parts from working. Cancer **cells** can break away from some types of tumor and spread to other parts of the body. Other types of tumor do not spread.

There are many different types of cancer. Some cancers affect a particular part of the body, such as the brain or the skin. **Leukemia** is a type of cancer that affects white blood cells in blood. The white blood cells of people with leukemia cannot fight off illness.

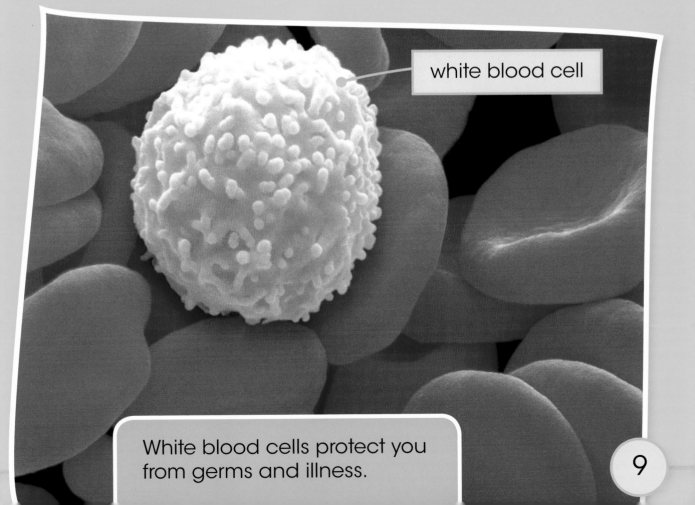

white blood cell

White blood cells protect you from germs and illness.

What Causes Cancer?

Smoking can cause some cancers.

Some cancers can be caused by smoking. Some may be caused by eating unhealthy food. However, the cause of many cancers is not known.

There are many ways to keep your body heathy and cut down the risk of getting cancer.

Stay healthy by:

- eating fewer fatty foods and more fruits and vegetables
- exercising every day to keep fit and healthy
- covering your skin and using sunscreen when you are in the sun
- trying not to stay in the sun for too long. Twenty minutes of sunshine is enough to keep your body healthy.

Understanding Cancer

If someone in your family has cancer, everyone feels worried. Some people die because their cancer is found too late and cannot be treated. But many people have treatment and survive.

There may be a lot to understand about possible treatments for cancer.

Scientists are working hard to find new and better ways to treat cancer.

When people talk about cancer, one word you might hear is "**remission**." This means that treatment has been successful and all signs of cancer are gone from the body.

Treating Cancer

Cancer can be treated by **surgery**, **chemotherapy**, or **radiation**. Sometimes one or all of the treatments are used. Surgery is when cancer **cells** are taken out of the body during an operation.

People are put into a very deep sleep before an operation so that they do not feel anything.

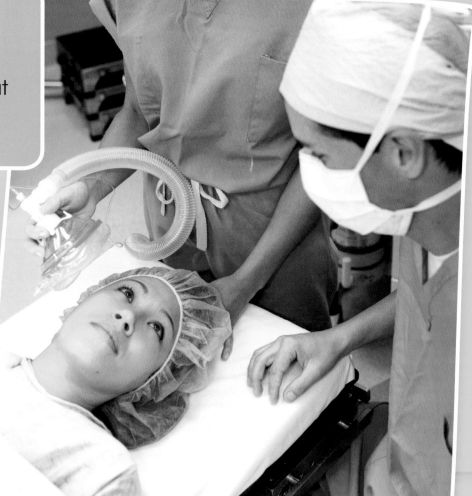

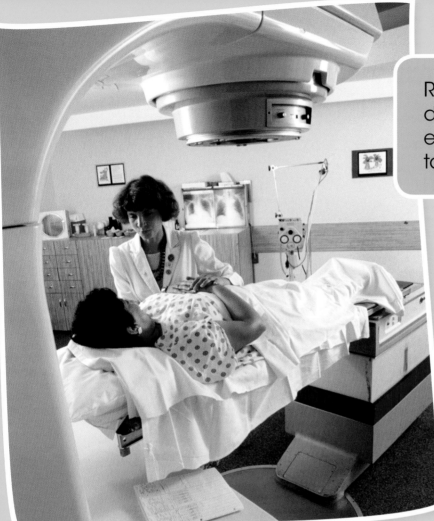

Radiation treatment does not hurt, and each treatment only takes a few minutes.

Radiation treatment uses special **energy** to kill cancer cells and stop **tumors** from growing. A radiation machine beams energy onto a part of the body to kill cancer cells.

Chemotherapy is a treatment in which medicine is put into the body to kill cancer **cells**. It is also used to try to stop cancer cells from growing or from coming back.

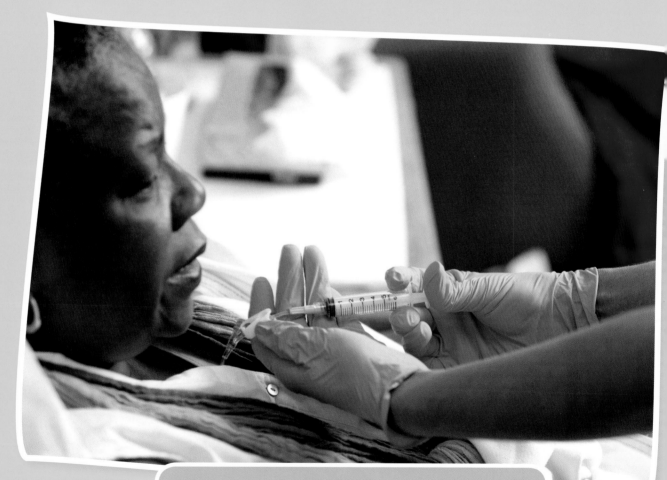

Chemotherapy and radiation are used with **surgery** to make sure all the cancer cells are destroyed.

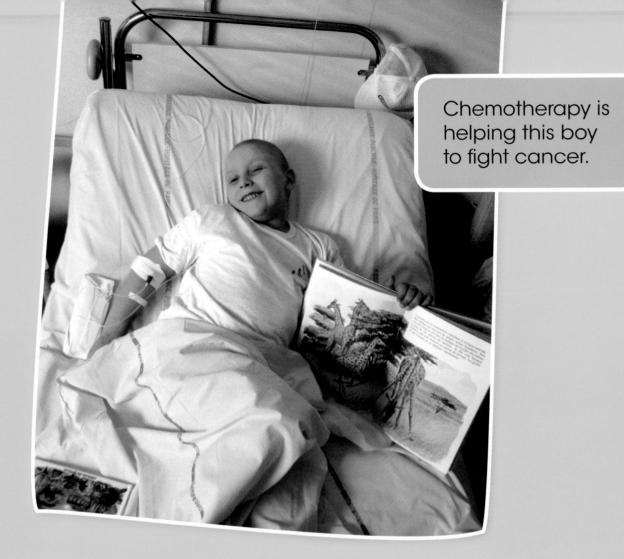

Chemotherapy is helping this boy to fight cancer.

People who have chemotherapy or **radiation** treatment may lose their hair, and they sometimes feel sick for a while. Their hair will grow back after the treatment has finished.

People who have had treatment may have to stay away from school or work for some time. This is because they are more likely to catch colds or other illnesses.

There are lots of ways to learn new things outside of school.

Many people make a strong recovery from cancer.

It can take a long time for life to get back to normal after treatment has finished. But most people who have had successful treatment are able to do all the things they did before.

How Does It Feel?

Talking about feelings and finding out that other people feel the same way can help.

Some people with cancer feel angry that they are sick. Sometimes people feel scared. It is important to understand that all these feelings are normal.

If you know someone close to you who has cancer, you may feel angry because he or she is sick and has to spend time in the hospital. You will probably be scared or worried, too.

You do not need to hide your feelings. It is okay to feel scared.

Being a Good Friend

If you know someone with cancer, try to be a good friend by treating your friend the same way you always have. Do not worry that you will not know what to do or say. Just take time to be together.

Find things that you enjoy doing together.

People with cancer may not want to talk about their illness. Everyone copes with illness in different ways.

Making plans will help you both look forward to the future.

Tips for helping a friend with cancer:
- Help your friend to stay cheerful. Make plans for things you can do together.
- Be there to listen if your friend wants to talk.

What Can I Do?

There are many different ways you can help people with cancer. For example, find out if there is anything you can do to help a family member who is having treatment. You may be able to help with jobs or take care of younger relatives.

Having help with everyday jobs can sometimes help people feel less anxious or scared.

Going on a sponsored walk can be a good way to raise money for charity.

Many **charities** work hard to raise money for cancer research. They use the money to try to find better treatment and **cures** for cancer. There are lots of different things you can do to help cancer charities.

Famous People with Cancer

Lance Armstrong is a famous cyclist. He found out he had cancer when he was 25. He had two **surgeries** and three rounds of **chemotherapy**. Lance started the Lance Armstrong Foundation to raise money for cancer research.

After his cancer treatment, Lance won the Tour de France, the world's most famous bike race, seven times.

Kylie Minogue is a supporter of the Pink Ribbon Foundation, which raises money for cancer research.

Kylie Minogue is a famous singer and actress. She found out that she had breast cancer in 2005. After surgery and a course of chemotherapy, she was in **remission**. This meant that all signs of cancer had been removed.

Cancer: True or False?

Sunscreen protects you from skin cancer.

TRUE! Sunscreen is helpful because it gives some protection against the harmful effects of the sun. It is also important not to stay in the sun for too long, and to keep skin covered up.

You can catch cancer from someone who has cancer.

FALSE! Cancer is not like a cold or flu. It cannot be passed from one person to another.

Everyone who gets cancer dies.

FALSE! Treatments for cancer are improving all the time. Many people make a very good recovery.

If your parents have cancer, then you will get cancer, too.

FALSE! Some cancers do run in families, but many do not. And even with cancers that do run in families, a person can do a lot to reduce the risk of getting cancer.

Glossary

cells smallest unit that makes up living things

charity organization that gives money or help to people who need it

chemotherapy using strong medicine to kill cancer cells

cure medical treatment that makes someone better

energy power that makes things move, change, or grow

leukemia type of cancer that stops white blood cells from doing their job of fighting illness

radiation treatment that uses special energy to kill cancer cells

remission time when a serious illness is better

surgery treatment involving opening up part of a person's body in order to repair something that is wrong

tumor swelling or lump caused by cells that grow in a way that is out of control

Find Out More

Books to Read

Fead, Beverlye Hyman, and Tessa Mae Hamermesh. *Nana, What's Cancer?* Atlanta: American Cancer Society, 2010.

Royston, Angela. *Cancer (What's It Like?)*. Chicago: Heinemann Library, 2005.

Websites

http://kidshealth.org/kid/health_problems/cancer/cancer.html
Visit Kids' Health to learn more about cancer.

www.cancer.org
Visit the American Cancer Society website, where you can find out more about cancer, its treatment, and more.

www.livestrong.org
The Lance Armstrong Foundation website is full of information and links to find out how to live with and beat cancer.

Index